Bad News First

The uncomfortable news you need to hear before the unbelievable news you'll want to hear

David Rotteveel

ISBN: 9781792888618

Dedication

For my beautiful wife, Stephanie, and our two wonderful children: Cadence and Luke.

Special "Thank you" to Mom & Dad, who have always supported and encouraged me.

To all whom The Lord has used to bring me along in the Faith.

CONTENTS

Introduction
The Dilemma All of Us Have Faced

So many of us have been confronted with the famous question:

"Do you want the good news first or the bad news first?"

What a dilemma!

I don't know how you answer this question, but for me, I want the bad news first every single time! If I have two pieces of news coming my way, one piece that is good and one that is bad, and certainly if I am given the choice, I want the bad news first. To be completely honest, I am not even sure exactly why I choose to hear the news this way. Maybe it's because I want to get the bad news out of the way so I no longer have it looming over my head... or maybe it's because I feel as though hearing the bad news will make the good news even better!

Have you ever heard someone mention or talk about something called the **Gospel of Jesus Christ**?

In the Bible, "Gospel" is defined in the original Greek language as euaggelion, which means "good news" or "good tidings." The Gospel is an announcement. And according to the Bible, it is **good news.** In fact, it is great news. Life-changing news. Transformational news. It is news that can raise the dead to life! How about that for good news? 'Good' seems like an understatement when you realize that the Gospel is news that, in itself, is "the power of God in salvation to those who believe" (Romans 1:16).

I heard a pastor say something once that struck a chord with me and immediately caused me to investigate the Scriptures to determine the validity and truth of his statement.

"The Gospel means good news. It is good news! It's all good! There is no bad news in it!" (I'm not telling you who said it.)

I was sitting front row in his "amen" section, cheering him on with passion and enthusiasm until his last statement. Here it is again:

"There is no bad news in the Gospel."

I understand what he was attempting to communicate. However, the truth is that there is bad news related to the Gospel, bad news that precedes the good news. **It's almost as though the good news isn't fully understood, or at the very least fully appreciated, until we hear the bad news.**

Here's my goal: I want to help us gain a new, more glorious appreciation of the good news of the Gospel of Jesus Christ.

As you begin to read this book, you likely have one of the following relationships with the Gospel:

- You have never heard it and have no familiarity with it.
- You have heard it but haven't quite come to fully understand it.
- You understand it and have responded to it but are not quite sure how it applies to your life as a Christian beyond the moment when you said "Yes" to Jesus.
- You have heard the Gospel in its entirety, properly responded to it, and are living in its power! If this describes you, may this book be a gentle reminder and a source of encouragement for you!

No matter where you stand with the Gospel, my prayer is that you will walk away with a greater love for this message of hope and ultimately realize that the Gospel is not just an introductory message into Christianity but rather the centerpiece of Christianity that sustains us as believers and motivates us throughout our entire journey with God.

That being said, before I can share the good news with you, I have to tell you the bad news first. Allow me to warn you: it's difficult to share and even more difficult to hear. Potentially, some of the things you are about to read have never been shared with you. Sadly, even if you have an extensive church background, you may find yourself angered and frustrated with some of the content you read in this book. I only ask that you consider my words within the context of the Scripture references and allow The Holy Spirit of God to teach, shape, and possibly even correct you.

I cannot emphasize enough how much I love you. Yes, you. Although we may never have met, my love for you is sincere, and my prayer for you is that this book would ultimately help you fall more in love with Jesus.

Chapter 1
The Bad News

Let's begin by talking about God.

The Bible is clear from beginning to end that there is one God. Although the common rhetoric of our culture is that there are many gods, we know that the God of the Bible has revealed Himself as the only God.

Deuteronomy 6:4 - The Lord our God, the Lord is one.

Isaiah 43:10 – "…I am He. Before me no god was formed, nor shall there be any after me."

Isaiah 44: 6 - Thus says the Lord, the King of Israel and his Redeemer, the Lord of hosts: "I am the first and I am the last; besides me there is no god."

There are hundreds of additional verses we could reference revealing the God we are discussing as the only God. The true God.

What else do we know about God from the Scriptures? We know that He is eternal.

Psalm 90:2 - Before the mountains were brought forth, or ever you had formed the earth and the world, from everlasting to everlasting, you are God.

Revelation 22:13 - "I am the Alpha and the Omega, the first and the last, the beginning and the end."

God is powerful. God is all-knowing. God is in control of all things. There are hundreds of characteristics or "attributes" of God we could discuss and thousands of Scriptures I could list. However, allow me to focus on one in particular.

God is good.

Sounds simple, right? You have likely heard the clich , "God is good all the time! And all the time God is good!" Most professing Christians have no issue with this statement. It has become widely, if not unanimously, accepted that the God of Christianity is viewed by Christians as good.

Allow me to suggest something. On its own, the truth that God is good is not good news. In fact, it's terrifying news.

Wait, did you just say it is bad news that God is good?

I did. Allow me to explain.

Paul Washer, a well-known pastor, author, and speaker, argues that the news of the goodness of God should scare us. It should terrify us.

But why? Why should any person tremble at the truth of the goodness of God?

Here's why. **People should be fearful of the goodness of God simply because people are not good.**

And herein lies the beginning of the bad news...
God is good, and people are not good. People are not innocent. People are not morally neutral. People are born, and even more appropriately, conceived, bad. Pure and simple; people are evil in nature.

Now, I am just going to assume that something fires up in you when I say that. Most people are offended when confronted with the reality that they are not morally pure or good. Why? Because, as humans, we have been conditioned to believe that "they" are bad. Who are "they"? Hitler, Stalin, the Nazis, outwardly racist people, people who participate in a certain sexual lifestyle, the people that belong to the opposite political party, the drug dealers, etc.

We have been deceived into believing that the world is divided into two kinds of people: "good people" and "bad people." As a culture, we have determined that whether or not a person is "good" or "bad" depends upon a set of factors such as upbringing, financial circumstance, or life choices. But, no matter what, the highest level of deception is believing that we, ourselves, are the "good" ones.

Here's the problem: The Bible knows nothing of these imaginary categories. It does not categorize mankind into "good" and "bad." The Bible presents a level playing field in which all human beings are in the same category: fallen, sinful, broken, wicked, evil.

Wait, did you just say that I'm "evil"?

I did. But I want to clarify two extremely important things. I also believe that I am evil. Also, I am not giving you my opinion... I am simply agreeing with what the Bible teaches.

I don't think the Bible teaches that at all!

Well, let's look at what the Bible says about our nature.

Genesis 6:5 & 8:21 - The Lord saw that the wickedness of man was great in the earth, and that every intention of the thoughts of his heart was only evil continually… from his youth.

Ecclesiastes 9:3 - Also, the hearts of the children of man are full of evil, and madness is in their hearts while they live, and after that they go to the dead.

2 Chronicles 6:36 - There is no one who does not sin.

Jeremiah 17:9 - The heart is deceitful above all things, and desperately sick; who can understand it?

Matthew 15:19 - For out of the heart come evil thoughts, murder, adultery, sexual immorality, theft, false witness, slander.

Romans 3, Psalm 14, Isaiah 53 - None is righteous, no, not one; no one understands; no one seeks for God. All have turned aside; together they have become worthless; no one does good, not even one.

Romans 3:23 - For all have sinned and fall short of the glory of God.

1 John 1:8,10 - If we say we have no sin, we deceive ourselves, and the truth is not in us. If we say we have not sinned, we make [God] a liar, and his word is not in us.

Believe me, I could keep going. In fact, I think I will...

The Apostle Paul, the man who is responsible for the authorship of more than half of the books in the New Testament, says in **Romans 7:18** – "For I know that nothing good dwells in me, that is, in my flesh."

Titus 3:3 - For we ourselves were once foolish, disobedient, led astray, slaves to various passions and pleasures, passing our days in malice and envy, hated by others and hating one another.

What does Jesus have to say on the subject? **Jesus says in John 8:34** - "Truly, truly, I say to you, everyone who commits sin is a slave to sin."

Take a moment and think about the imagery that comes to mind when you think of "slavery." A few things are true of a slave: a slave is in bondage to the will of the Master, a slave has no freedom, and a slave cannot decide to no longer be a slave but must be granted freedom by an act of the Master.

So, what do we know? We know that naturally, we are bound, and even enslaved by, a corrupted sinful nature.

Potentially, at one time or another, you heard a pastor label a certain sexual sin as an **abomination** to the Lord. In that moment, you may have exhaled a sigh of relief because you were innocent of that specific offense. It's a clever way we can divert attention and buy into the lie that we are safe and "good" because we have not committed one of a few actions that are labelled as "abominations."

Please understand. I am not saying I disagree that certain sexual behaviors are an abomination. But, if we're being honest, **most evangelicals love to expose the sin of others in a strategic attempt to disguise or distract from their own sin.** Again, regarding certain sins being an abomination to The Lord, I don't believe less than that, I believe more than that.

Proverbs 15:9 - The way of the wicked is an **abomination** to the Lord.

Proverbs 15:8 - The sacrifice of the wicked is an **abomination** to the Lord.

Proverbs 28:9 - If one turns away his ear from hearing the law, even his prayer is an **abomination**.

No, no, no! You don't know me! I have done a lot of good!

Yes, this is the tragic lie that I believed for years and years. In my mind, it was as though there were scales. The opposite ends of the scales represented my "good" and "bad" actions. So, every time I lied (or at least got caught in a lie), a weight was dropped on the "bad" side. But then, every time I volunteered at a nursing home or prayed aloud before a meal, a weight was dropped on the "good" side, thus balancing the scales. I was putting all of my hope into a myth. Here is the myth (actually, a lie) that I believed for a large part of my life: **If there is a God, He will probably weigh my good against my bad and, even if it's close, He will probably cut me a break because no matter what my scale looks like, at least I'm not a murderer or Hitler or anyone like that!**

I was 17 years old and several years into believing and living under the porous roof of this awful delusion when a friend of mine sent me a YouTube clip of a sermon preached by Mark Driscoll. Driscoll is the former Lead Pastor/Founder of Mars Hill Church in Seattle, Washington, and current Lead Pastor/Founder of The Trinity Church in Scottsdale, Arizona. The sermon was about Biblical manhood. I enjoyed it tremendously. However, one of the related videos was a clip from a sermon in which Driscoll explained the tragic reality of God's perception of my "good" deeds.

He explained that God was disgusted by my "good" deeds and my self-righteousness. This came as a huge shock to me. I had never heard it explained to me like he explained it. He quoted and explained Isaiah 64:6:

Isaiah 64:6 - We have all become like one who is unclean, and **all our righteous deeds are like a polluted garment.**

This simple statement by Isaiah, echoed throughout the New Testament, even by Jesus Himself, summarizes exactly how God feels about your and my self-righteousness. He perceives our righteousness like one would perceive a used tissue or, more specific to the text, a female hygiene product. Simply put, He is not pleased. Furthermore, He is disgusted by it (our self-righteousness). He rejects it. He does not accept it.

Dude, you are bumming me out!

Hang in there. It gets worse before it gets better! But I sincerely believe that we must understand the severity of our situation before we can understand the beauty of what Jesus has done. **We must realize the magnitude of our sin before we can celebrate the magnificence of our Savior!**

Takeaways from Chapter 1

We must realize the magnitude of our sin before we can celebrate the magnificence of our Savior!

Popular lie that many believe: If there is a God, He will probably weigh my good against my bad and, even if it's close, He will probably cut me a break because no matter what my scale looks like, at least I'm not a murderer or Hitler or anything like that!

Most evangelicals love to expose the sin of others in a strategic attempt to disguise or distract from their own sin.

People should be fearful of the goodness of God simply because people are not good.

It's almost as though the good news isn't fully understood, or at the very least fully appreciated, until we hear the bad news.

Chapter 2
God Does Not Grade Like a School Teacher, He Rules Like a Judge

Perhaps a helpful distinction would be to note the difference between a school teacher and a judge. A school teacher issues many judgments, thus the essence of teaching. Most people, and unfortunately even some Christians, view God as a school teacher. We sort of view life as some sort of cosmic test, like we are working toward a final grade. And in this cosmic test, much like in school, a "C" will work just fine. So, there's plenty of room to make some mistakes and be crazy as long as we level ourselves out in the end. Perhaps, along the way, we score some bonus points by attending church once in a while, listening to some worship music, memorizing some Bible verses, or helping one of our friends move.

However, the Bible does not portray God as a school teacher but as a judge. (See Psalm 75:7, Psalm 50:6, Isaiah 33:22, 2 Timothy 4:8, Hebrews 12:23, James 4:12, and about 70 more references.)

What do we know about judges? Well, we know that judges do not issue grades but verdicts. What are the two verdicts that a judge can render? Innocent or guilty.

I always cringe when someone yells, often in self-defense, "Only God can judge me!!!" I'm a local church pastor, and I hear that a lot. My response is always the same: "I agree with you...100%...however, don't you want to know **how** He is going to judge you?"

God doesn't judge us based on our broken standard but based upon His perfect standard. Please allow me to cut right to the chase.

Here's the reality: All of us, on our own, standing before God, are guilty. We are not graded on different scales but rather rendered a just verdict. And that verdict is guilty.

I am aware that most people believe themselves to be innocent according to their own standard of morality and ethics. Most people do not consider themselves to be guilty in any sense. But the Bible is clear that those who break God's Law are guilty.

Dude, how can you say I'm guilty of anything? You don't even know me!

You're right, I don't. But I do share one thing in common with you. I am a human. You know what I know about you without even knowing you? I know you've lied. In fact, I would venture to say that you probably can't even recall how many lies you've told throughout the course of your life. Now, what do you call someone who can't even count how many lies they have told? Come on, you can say it. Admit it. Still don't want to? Let's put it this way: I'm sure there are people in your life who have lied to you once, just once, and you have forever labelled them a liar. You know what that means? You're a liar.

You have also stolen things. That makes you a thief.

Yeah, I've made mistakes, but so has everyone else! We have ALL done that stuff!!!

I know. But allow me to press you on that point. If you were driving down the road traveling 50 miles per hour over the speed limit, thus breaking the law, you would be guilty of breaking the law. Now, imagine a police officer pulls you over. Do you think you could convince the cop that you were innocent because you're not the only person to have ever exceeded the speed limit? You see how that doesn't make any sense? **The truth that others are guilty along with you does not change the reality that you are guilty as well.**

What do guilty people deserve? Punishment, right? It's hard to find someone, especially in America, who would disagree with the notion that people who break the law are worthy to be punished. What does it say about our culture as Americans that legal and crime dramas are among the most popular genres of television? We are all in favor of the notion: protect the innocent, **punish the guilty**.

One thing that is blindingly true of Americans is that we are completely supportive of justice for the guilty unless we, ourselves, happen to be guilty...then there is a deafening plea for mercy followed by a laundry list of excuses and a defense for why we had an appropriate reason to be guilty.

And, just in case you think anyone might be exempt from certain Laws, and thus, able to avoid the consequences of their guilt, **James 2:10** points out, "For whoever keeps the whole law and **yet stumbles in one point, he has become guilty of all.**"

So, I ask in love, can we please stop pretending that the problem is "out there" and face the sobering reality that the problem is within? As someone once said, **"The heart of the problem is the problem of the heart."**

The Punishment Should Fit the Crime

As human beings, we are guilty of breaking God's Law. Here's the conclusion: since God is eternal and holy, it means our offense against Him is a big deal. Treason against the eternal God demands and even requires eternal punishment. As criminals, we are fully deserving of the wrath of God. One could make the argument that until people understand and agree with this truth, they have yet to comprehend the Gospel of Jesus Christ.

There is a place reserved for people who are guilty of sin and who die in their sin. That place is called "Hell." Hell is not a place for the "bad" people while Heaven exists for the "good" people. Hell is not a place of fun, partying lawlessness. Hell is a real place where real people will go for eternity. Hell is the wrath of God in effect. Hell is where justice is perfectly served on those who reject God and die in their sin as guilty criminals. Hell is what we all deserve.

You can't possibly believe this!

Oh, I do. I absolutely believe that I am worthy of nothing but the wrath of God. If God were to take my life right now and I were to go to Hell, that would not make God unjust or unfair. **Hell and the wrath of God are precisely what I deserve, and apart from Christ, are exactly what I would have received.** It is exactly what would have happened to me had Christ not intervened. (Much more on this later!!!)

Takeaways from Chapter 2

Hell and the wrath of God are precisely what I deserve,
and apart from Christ, are exactly what I would have
received.

"The heart of the problem is the problem of the heart."

The truth that others are guilty along with you does not
change the reality that you are guilty as well.

One thing that is blindingly true of Americans is that we are completely supportive of justice for the guilty unless we, ourselves, happen to be guilty...then there is a deafening plea for mercy followed by a laundry list of excuses and a defense for why we had an appropriate reason to be guilty.

Chapter 3
Horribly Unable

So often, in modern-American "spiritual" culture, the response is something like: I can fix this on my own! No one can tell me what I can and cannot do! I will just pull myself up from the boot straps and white-knuckle life as I strive for a higher level of morality! If God wants me to be better, I'll be better!

That's the problem. Christianity is not a system for changing people from "bad" to "good." If I may be so bold: **Any "Christians" who believe that belonging to Christianity makes them superior to anyone else have excluded themselves from Biblical Christianity with that horrific belief alone.** When one becomes a Christian, he or she does not become "good" but alive! (See Ephesians 2:1-10)

This problem is not solved by simply adding a little bit of religion in our lives to round ourselves out. JD Greear, Pastor of The Summit Church and current President of the Southern Baptist Convention, said it best: "Jesus did not come as a life coach to help us turn over a new leaf. Jesus comes as a resurrected Savior to give us a new life."

The problem is that we are dead (yes, literally dead) in our trespasses and sins according to Ephesians 2:1, and we are in need of someone to raise us to life. This is something we are **incapable** of doing on our own.

Look at **Romans 8:7** - For the mind that is set on the flesh is hostile to God, for it does not submit to God's Law; indeed, it **cannot**.

We cannot submit to God's Law while we are separated from God. **Because we are truly dead in our sin, we are incapable and unable to obey our way into God's presence.**

At this point, the common objection from people is this: Well, what about the Law? God gave us rules to obey and follow to become better people and live a better life!

No. He didn't. If your understanding of God's Law is anything similar to the above synopsis, then I say this with the utmost love and humility: you have no understanding of God's Law.

Then what is the point of the Law? **God gave us His Law to reveal His standard of absolute righteousness in order to convict us all of our true guilt before Him so that we would see our need for a Savior.**

Takeaways from Chapter 3

Any "Christians" who believe that belonging to Christianity makes them superior to anyone else have excluded themselves from Biblical Christianity with that horrific belief alone.

This problem (our sin which separates us from God) is not solved by simply adding a little bit of religion in our lives to round ourselves out as a person.

Because we are truly dead in our sin, we are incapable and unable to obey our way into God's presence.

God gave us His Law to reveal His standard of absolute righteousness in order to convict us all of our true guilt before Him so that we would see our need for a Savior.

Chapter 4

A Journey Through Romans 3

Let's allow God's Word to speak for itself as we walk through a portion of God's Word together.

In Romans 3, The Apostle Paul, under the inspiration of the Holy Spirit (2 Peter 1:21), gives us a glorious understanding of the problem of our nature and the glory of God's grace through Christ! The Apostle Paul begins his argument in verse 10 by quoting from Psalm 14 and 53 in the Old Testament: **"As it is written: none is righteous, no, not one; no one understands; no one seeks for God."**

No one is righteous. No one understands. No one seeks for God. "I was saved because I was seeking for God and found Him!" Lovingly, that is an error. If you are saved, you are saved because God sought after you and found you. It was you who were lost.

Romans 3:12 - All have turned aside; together they have become worthless; no one does good, not even one.

As I mentioned previously, I used to rest in the hope that God would take my "good deeds" into account. I hoped that God would weigh my good and bad actions on a scale and, if my good were to outweigh my bad, He would let me into Heaven (if He and Heaven even existed). But God exposed that error in my thinking through His Word and helped me to understand the reality of this passage along with dozens and dozens like it.

Romans 3:13-17 - Their throat is an open grave; they use their tongues to deceive. The venom of asps is under their lips. Their mouth is full of curses and bitterness. Their feet are swift to shed blood; in their paths are ruin and misery, and the way of peace they have not known.

Romans 3:18 - There is no fear of God before their eyes.

As fallen beings, we have no fear of God. And yet, we must fear God. This isn't to mean that we ought to be afraid of God, but we should be in awe of His majesty and power. When we think of God, we should feel weak and powerless compared to His strength and might. However, because we have been utterly corrupted by sin, the opposite is often true. When we think of God, we like to believe our strength is comparable and our will is stronger because after all, God would never impose His will on almighty man! Again, we believe this falsely. A proper understanding of God would help us gain a more proper understanding of ourselves.

Romans 3:19 - Now we know that whatever the law says it speaks to those who are under the law, so that every mouth may be stopped, and the whole world may be held accountable to God.

Did you catch that? What does God's Law do? It was given so that "every mouth may be stopped." In other words, the Law was given so that we have nothing to say when it exposes our sin. Our defense completely falls apart. **When the Law, which is a portrait of perfection, is held up, our claim to be "good enough"** or **"strong enough"** or **"moral enough" collapses**. Look again at the final phrase of the verse: **"...and the whole word may be held accountable to God."**

We are held accountable. **The blinding reality is this: we are not the standard, and we are not free to determine the standard.** I know that when you compare yourself to the criminals on the evening news and the prisoners on death row, you are awesome in your own mind. The problem is, you have the wrong standard. The standard is perfection. Take your moral resume and your silly list of "good deeds" and line them up against perfection. How do you compare? As we are about to see, you fall short.

Romans 3:20 - For by works of the law no human being will be justified in his sight, since through the law comes knowledge of sin.

"Justified" simply means "saved." How are you going to justify your sin? You have your reasons ready? Excuses locked and loaded? Perhaps you'll attempt to use that cowardly tactic of diverting attention from your sins to the few times you made the right choices? Are you planning on trying to convince God that you kept His Law? **The point of the Law is not to save you but to prove to you that you need to be saved!**

Romans 3:21 - But now the righteousness of God has been manifested apart from the law, although the Law and the Prophets bear witness to it—

There is so much beauty in this verse!

Righteousness...perfection...justification...salvation has been manifested or achieved apart from the Law! Not through the Law, but apart from it! The Law of God has not accomplished anything on its own. It has merely shown us that righteousness on our own is un-accomplishable.

Romans 3:22 - The righteousness of God through faith in Jesus Christ for all who believe

"The righteousness of God", not the righteousness of man. This is an absolutely crucial distinction. **It's not about our righteousness, it's about His. You don't need your broken definition of "good enough." You need God's perfect righteousness.**

How do we get it? Through faith. Through faith! Ephesians 2 makes a distinction between faith and works when Paul writes that it is by grace we have been saved, through faith. He even clarifies again to say that we have not been saved as a result of works in case anyone might boast. (See Ephesians 2:1-10, namely verses 8-9.)

Romans 3:22-25 - For there is no distinction: For all have sinned and fall short of the glory of God,

All. Including you. Including me.

and are justified by his grace as a gift, through the redemption that is in Christ Jesus...

Justified (saved) by God's grace. Grace is to represent something we do not deserve. Let me clarify once again. Everything God has done for us has been done not because we are awesome but because He (God) is awesome.

whom God put forward as a propitiation by his blood, to be received by faith.

Propitiation is a big word that simply means: God's wrath is satisfied. His anger toward sin was totally and completely appeased and the payment due for our sin was paid in full and accepted when Jesus died on the cross! And again, salvation is to be received freely, not achieved, by faith in Christ alone.

Romans 3:25-26 - This was to show God's righteousness, because in his divine forbearance he had passed over former sins. It was to show his righteousness at the present time, so that he might be just and the justifier of the one who has faith in Jesus.

Since God is the only one Who is just and righteous, He is the only One who can justify us and declare us righteous.

Romans 3:27-28 - Then what becomes of our boasting? It is excluded. By what kind of law? By a law of works? No, but by the law of faith. For we hold that one is justified by faith apart from works of the law.

You and I have nothing to boast about. This is why, as a preacher of the Gospel, I discourage boasting. And also why as a follower of Christ, I (imperfectly) ask for accountability when pride begins to manifest itself in my life. I have been saved and declared righteous and justified because of the unmerited favor of God. I have been saved by His grace alone and not only am I undeserving (which would imply that I could somehow deserve it), I am ill-deserving (which means I deserve much, much worse).

Takeaways from Chapter 4

When the Law, which is a portrait of perfection, is held up...our claim to be "good enough" or "strong enough" or "moral enough" completely collapses.

The point of the Law is not to save you but to prove to you that you need to be saved!

It's not about our righteousness, it's about His. You don't need your broken definition of "good enough." You need God's perfect righteousness.

Since God is the only one Who is just and righteous, He is the only One who can justify someone and declare them righteous.

Chapter 5
A Summary

God is good. People are not.

God is holy, righteous, perfect and good. You and I are imperfect, selfish, sinful, and corrupted by a sinful nature.

Because we are sinners, we are guilty of breaking God's Law.

God is perfectly within His Divine right to punish those who are guilty according to the perfect standard of His Law.

You and I, as guilty criminals before God, deserve nothing other than the righteous wrath of God.

There is no way to avoid this reality on our own. We can't be good enough on our own. We can't try hard enough, we can't prescribe to a religion or a system of ethics, we can't give enough money or do enough good to outweigh our bad. It's impossible.

So, wait a minute, are you saying that we are completely and utterly helpless and hopeless on our own?

Are you saying that I am so bad that I deserve Hell?

Are you saying there's nothing I can do to save myself?

Yes. That is exactly what I'm saying.

Chapter 6

The Good News

You did it!!! You made it through the bad news! Now, onto the good and glorious news!

Christianity is centered around a message called "the Gospel of Jesus Christ." As I mentioned earlier, the word "gospel" comes from the Greek word, euaggelion meaning "good news" or "glad tidings." **The Gospel is a proclamation or a glorious announcement. What is the announcement? The announcement is the good news of what God has done in the person and work of Jesus Christ!**

We spent the first half of this book discussing the reality, albeit a difficult and often painful reality, that we

39

all face as fallen, sin-diseased human beings. Now, we are going to move on to discuss the remedy - the magnificent, hope-filled, joyous remedy to our common problem as sinners separated from a good and holy God, our Creator.

The Good News begins with God.

As we have already established, there is One God. God, as revealed in Scripture, is the Creator, Sustainer, and Lord of all things. **God is self-defining, self-sustaining, and self-sufficient.**

God is self-defining, meaning that God is the One who defines who He is. As human beings, it is not up to us to define God. Because of the corruption of sin, which produces pride in us, we often fall into the trap of believing that it is up to us to define who God is. I'm sure you have probably heard (or read on social media) something like this:

"I like to think of God like a..."

"What is God like? Well, the way I see it..."

"I could never believe in a God who would..."

You may have even said something like that. Because, quite honestly, we all have believed these things in some shape or form. We must remember that God is the Creator, and we are His creation, made in God's own image. **This means that God determines and defines who we are, not the other way around.**

God is self-sustaining. Why did God create us? Some say it was because God was lonely and wanted fellowship. This could not be farther from the truth. God, as He is revealed in Scripture, is not lonely, lacking, or in need. God is not desperate for human interaction. God needs nothing in order to exist.

Hebrews 1:3 - And He (Jesus) is the radiance of His glory and the exact representation of His nature, and **upholds all things by the word of His power**.

Did you catch that? We are being sustained and held together by Jesus, not the other way around.

God is self-sufficient. God was not created. God did not come into existence. God is not threatened by anyone or anything. God is perfectly sufficient. God is enough.

God is the Creator of all things. It was out of the overflow of His own perfection that God created mankind in His image and likeness with dignity, value, worth, and purpose. The purpose for which He created us was to worship Him and enjoy Him forever. (See the Westminster Shorter Catechism.) We were created by God, not in order to keep God company or provide fellowship for God, but in order to glorify Him!

But rather than abiding with God and fulfilling this purpose for which we were created, we entered into rebellion against God and committed treason against Him by choosing to turn our worship away from God and toward ourselves (see Romans 1). Because we are sinners by nature and choice, we are separated from God with no way back.

However, the Bible is consistent from cover to cover in revealing to us one incredible, life-giving truth. **God is most passionate about His own glory. God's glory and fame are utmost on His list of priorities and desires.** Out of this desire, God sent His Son "to seek and save the lost" (Luke 19:10). Another way to say this would be that God took on flesh.

Quick side note: I would love to spend more time on the Doctrine of the Trinity, that is, the specifics of God's

Nature. However, I am going to continue discussing the actions of God and would highly encourage you to go to Amazon.com and purchase "The Forgotten Trinity", a synopsis on the Triune Nature of God, written by Dr. James White. I could not recommend it more highly.

This is where Jesus comes in! Jesus Christ was the One, True, and Eternal God in human form (John 1). Jesus is the exact imprint of God's nature (Hebrews 1:3). Jesus was fully and truly God (Colossians 1:15-21). Jesus did not come to simply show attention to the outcasts and marginalized of society. Jesus did not come to show us some interesting magic tricks or "divine sleight of hand." Jesus did not come to introduce a new philosophy or even begin a religion. Jesus came for a specific purpose. **Jesus' purpose, as summarized in Scripture, was to live by upholding the law of God (Matthew 5:17) and to die under the wrath of God (Acts 2:23), in order to reconcile people to God (Colossians 1:20) for the glory of God (John 12).**

That's a lot. Let's break it down.

Jesus made it clear that He was from God (John 10:33). While on Earth, Jesus was God in bodily form. He was the eternal Son of God wrapped in flesh. He was not a mere moral teacher or an intelligent philosopher. Jesus was the Creator God who took on flesh and dwelt among His people (John 1:14).

As you continue, please don't forget the significance of Jesus' identity. **A failure to understand who Jesus was is the quickest way to undervalue the things that He said and did.**

Jesus came from God in order to uphold the Law of God. Jesus, being God in the flesh, was perfectly obedient (Philippians 2:8). Jesus perfectly and sufficiently obeyed the Law of God. Jesus never sinned. He was tempted in every way, as we are, yet He was completely without sin (Luke 4, Hebrews 4). Jesus was completely righteous, blameless, spotless, sinless, and perfect. It is important to remember that the reason for Jesus' sinlessness was because of His nature. Allow me to expound…

You and I do not become sinners because we sin. You and I sin because we are sinners. Do you see the difference? It could be compared to symptoms of the flu. You don't get the flu because you coughed, sneezed, and experienced aches, pains and a fever. Those are merely symptoms of someone who has the flu. In other words, you don't begin with symptoms, you begin with sickness. Symptoms are the by-product of the sickness, and medical professionals are often able to diagnose a person's sickness based on his or her symptoms. The reason we show symptoms of sinful behavior is because of our sickness, which is our sinful nature. **We don't become sinners because we sin, we sin because we are sinners.**

Jesus is different. Completely different. **Jesus did not become God because He didn't sin. Jesus didn't sin because He was and is God. Jesus was not a perfect man who became a god, but rather, He is the perfect God who became a man.** Jesus' nature was one of purity, righteousness, and holiness. Despite being wrapped in flesh and clothed in humanity, Jesus' nature was sinless and, out of His nature, came perfect obedience.

You know, people often misrepresent Jesus. Unfortunately, there was overwhelming confusion as to who Jesus was while He walked the earth, which means that it should not come as a surprise that there is still much confusion over His identity today.

In all of the false representations and incorrect statements concerning Jesus, one thing that people rarely take into consideration is **why** He died. Let's remember, Jesus was murdered by the Roman Government (in partnership with the Jewish leaders, Jesus' own people), as an Enemy of the State and sentenced to the worst form of punishment in that day (death by crucifixion). Why? Because he introduced a new philosophy? Because he healed people? Because he started a religion? No. **Jesus was crucified because He openly, publicly, repeatedly, emphatically, and unapologetically claimed to be God. (John 5:8, John 8:58, Mark 14:61-62). He also claimed to have the ability to forgive sin (Luke 5:20) and performed miracles that demonstrated His power over life and death (John 11).**

So, Jesus is executed for a crime called blasphemy. The Roman soldiers of his day stripped him naked, beat Him, and flogged Him. They ironically shoved a crown of thorns on Jesus' head and beat it into His skull. They drove nine-inch nails through each of His hands and through both of His feet simultaneously. They did all of this publicly, as a spectacle. They left Him hanging on the cross to suffocate and bleed to death. After ensuring His death by stabbing Him through the side with a spear, they placed Him in a tomb where He remained for three days. He then rose again from the dead, conquering sin, death, Hell, and the grave, and thus displayed His power and dominion over all things.

Jesus lived the perfect life that we need but are incapable of living. He died the death that we were condemned to die because of our sin, and He rose again from the dead in order to raise us to new life in Him.

Who Jesus is and what He did is perfectly sufficient for salvation and faith in Him is the only hope that anyone has to be reunited and reconciled to God.

Takeaways from Chapter 6

God determines and defines who we are, not the other way around.

God is self-defining, self- sustaining, and self-sufficient.

Jesus did not become God because He didn't sin. Jesus didn't sin because He was and is God. Jesus was not a perfect man who became a god, but rather, He is the perfect God who became a man.

A failure to understand who Jesus was is the quickest way to undervalue the things that He said and did.

Jesus was crucified because He openly, publicly, repeatedly, emphatically and unapologetically claimed to be God. (John 5:8, John 8:58, Mark 14:61-62). He also claimed to have the ability to forgive sin (Luke 5:20) and performed miracles that demonstrated His power over life and death (John 11).

We don't become sinners because we sin, we sin because we are sinners.

Jesus did not become God because He didn't sin. Jesus didn't sin because He was and is God. Jesus was not a perfect man who became a god, but rather, He is the perfect God who became a man.

Jesus lived the perfect life that we need but are incapable of living. He died the death that we were condemned to die because of our sin and He rose again from the dead in order to raise us to new life in Him.

Who Jesus is and what He did is perfectly sufficient for salvation and faith in Him is the only hope that anyone has to be reunited and reconciled to God.

Chapter 7

My Confession

Can I be honest? I spent a long time afraid to admit
something. There was a question I couldn't answer. I
even participated in church activities, attended youth
group, volunteered in different ministries, and put
"Christian" in the "About Me" section of my Facebook
page while struggling with a serious question. It was one
of those situations where I felt as though too much time
had passed, and therefore, I would be humiliated if
anyone knew that I didn't know the answer to this
question. Here was the question:

What in the world does Jesus dying on the cross have to do with me?

Yes, Jesus is God. Got it.

He died on the cross for me. Okay, sure.

On the third day, He rose again from the dead. I accept that.

It wasn't the order of events that confused me or even whether or not they were true. I believed all of the above statements. I simply couldn't connect the pieces. Jesus died…and it was for me? How does that work? Why is that necessary? I thought it was awesome, but I had no idea how it really worked.

I can't explain to you what happened to me emotionally, physically, and spiritually when The Holy Spirit finally revealed to me the answer to this question. It completely wrecked my life. Following Jesus became a delight and was no longer a duty. Everything changed.

I'll never forget the moment God opened my eyes to the majesty and wonder and provided a glimpse of His glory when He revealed this to me: **Jesus did not just die <u>for</u> me. He died <u>instead</u> of me.**

This completely changed my life. Everything clicked. It made sense. Jesus died instead of me. This meant that He hung in my place. He died as though He were me.

Perhaps you're smarter than me (and you probably are). But let me tell you a quick, simple story to show you the wonder of this reality. My prayer is that, by God's grace, something clicks in you and The Holy Spirit invades your heart and mind like He did mine.

A few months ago, my pastor approached me and said he had a question for me. His question: "David, can you preach for me at the end of the month?" It's a seemingly straightforward question. Let me call you to a word in the middle of the question: "David, can you preach **for** me…?" In reality, what was he truly asking me? He was asking me to preach **instead** of him. He was asking me to replace him (temporarily). He was asking me to stand in his place and serve **as a substitute** for him.

What makes Jesus' death on the cross significant is that His death was our death to die. When Jesus died, He didn't simply die for you, although that is absolutely true. Jesus died instead

of you. He died as though He were you. He died as you.

When Jesus died, He absorbed the punishment from God that you and I deserve. Earlier, I argued that guilty people deserve punishment and also that the punishment should fit the crime. As criminals who are guilty of breaking the Law of God, we deserve to die and experience the fullness of His righteous wrath and anger toward our sin and rebellion. When Jesus died on the cross, He died by hanging in our place. While on that cross, Jesus experienced the fullness of God's righteous wrath and anger toward sin. Make no mistake, I understand that even popular Christian movies attribute Jesus' death to Satan as though Satan killed Jesus. Satan did not kill Jesus. God killed Jesus. God the Father gave up His Son, and Jesus served as the perfect sacrifice for sin while completely appeasing the wrath of God. **Jesus did not die because He was guilty, He died because we are guilty. Jesus died the criminal's death, not because He was a criminal, but because we are criminals.**

1 Peter 3:18 - For Christ also suffered for sins once for all, **the righteous for the unrighteous,** to bring you to God.

There it is. The righteous in place of the unrighteous. The innocent in place of the guilty. The just in place of the unjust. The Perfect in place of the imperfect. God in place of His people.

What is the result according to 1 Peter 3:18? To bring you to God. Let me reiterate, lovingly. You can't bring yourself to God. We can't solve this problem on our own because we are the problem. Because you and I caused the problem by virtue of our sin, we cannot solve this problem or overcome our sin. The wonderful news of the Gospel is that Jesus solved this problem. Jesus is called "the Christ." You know what "Christ" means? It means that Jesus is the "anointed one" and the "chosen one." Ultimately, It means that Jesus Christ was chosen and anointed to be the ultimate solution to sin and death. Jesus, Himself, is the solution to sin and death.

And there's more!

Not only did Jesus take all of our sin and absorb the wrath of God that was meant for you and for me. Not only did He die in our place and pay the penalty that we owed. Not only did He take our guilt, shame, and sin then die as though it were His own, but He also gives us His perfect righteousness!

Martin Luther, the patriarch of the Protestant Reformation, referred to this as the "great exchange." **Jesus took the punishment that was ours and gave us His righteousness, something He alone is worthy of. God trades our rap sheet of crimes for Jesus' resume of perfection. We give God our sin; God gives us Himself.**

2 Corinthians 5:21 - For our sake he made him to be sin who knew no sin, so that in him we might become the righteousness of God.

This means that I am perfectly justified by God because of the person and work of Jesus Christ. **God did not ignore my sin; He punished Jesus for my sin.** It is not that I have escaped justice, but rather, the justice meant for me was thrown upon Jesus. The truth remains: justice for sin will take place either at the cross of Christ or in Hell. The reality is this: either you will pay for and be punished for your sin or you will trust that what Jesus did on the cross was sufficient to pay for your sin.

Romans 3:26 - It was to show his righteousness at the present time, so that he might be just and the justifier of the one who has faith in Jesus.

Takeaways from Chapter 7

What makes Jesus' death on the cross significant is that His death was our death to die. When Jesus died, He didn't simply die for you, although that is absolutely true. Jesus died instead of you. He died as though He were you. He died as you.

Jesus didn't die because He was guilty, He died because we are guilty. Jesus died the criminal's death, not because He was a criminal, but because we are criminals.

Jesus took the punishment that we were worthy of and we are given Jesus' righteousness that He alone is worthy of. God trades our rap sheet of crimes for Jesus' resume of perfection. We give God our sin, God gives us Himself.

God did not ignore my sin, but He punished Jesus for my sin.

Justice will be served for sin, either at the cross or in Hell.

Chapter <u>8</u>
Part of the Cupcake

Spending time with my children is, by far, one of my favorite things to do. At the risk of sounding like a typical "dad", I must say that my daughter (6) is beautiful, brilliant, and one of the funniest, joy-filled people that I know.

Once, she and I did a "My Little Pony" puzzle together. I must say, as embarrassing as this is, she was slightly quicker than me at finding pieces to the puzzle. I remember thinking how thankful I am that she primarily takes after her mother.

As we were finishing the puzzle, we realized we were missing one piece. We looked around for a moment and couldn't find it. My daughter knew from the box that the missing piece was part of a cupcake. To be honest, a piece missing from the puzzle bothered me far more than it bothered her. I have never been diagnosed with OCD, but then again, I have never been tested. The missing cupcake piece truly bothered me!

Similarly, there is a piece to the puzzle of the Gospel that is often left out. I'm not sure it is left out intentionally; however, I would suggest that finding this piece not only helps us complete the message of the Gospel but also gives us a more spectacular love for it!

Here's the piece:

God did not do all He has done for us because we are His friends. God did all He has done for us despite us being His enemies.

Before any follower of Christ becomes a follower of Christ, he or she was an enemy of God.

Romans 5:10 - For if while we were enemies we were reconciled to God by the death of his Son, much more, now that we are reconciled, shall we be saved by his life.

Romans 8:7 - The mind governed by the flesh is hostile to God; it does not submit to God's law, nor can it do so.

Colossians 1:21 - Once you were alienated from God and were enemies in your minds...

By nature of our sin, we are not only separated from God, but we are hostile toward Him and set ourselves against Him as His enemies.

In movies and storylines, rebellion is often celebrated and deemed heroic. Poor, marginalized, mistreated people rise up in rebellion against the evil powers-that-be. I have personally sat in movie theaters and found myself cheering for the lowly, the underdog, the abused, in hopes that they would ultimately overthrow their wicked oppressors.

But our rebellion against God was quite different. God is not an evil tyrant but a generous, loving Father. God is overflowing with grace and mercy. His character or essence is one of love and compassion. All of His glorious attributes are marked by goodness. Thus, our rebellion against Him is incomprehensible! It is maddening to think that we entered a rebellion against this truly wonderful God. There was no oppression being forced upon us; there was no neglect or abuse from God toward us. If we were to take a moment and think back to Adam and Eve, what could we gather? Adam and Eve were at peace with God. Their needs were perfectly provided. They had direct and unhindered communication with God. They enjoyed perfect communion with their Creator. Before sin entered the world, there was no enmity, no rivalry between man and God. The treason committed by Adam and Eve, and ultimately mankind, comes out of a rebellious spirit. Adam and Eve may have disobeyed in their actions, but their attitude is what caused them (and the entire human race thereafter) to become enemies of God.

Paul begins his letter to the Roman church by giving us an understanding of the heart behind our sin and folly. He is trying to attack the underlying issue and not simply its effects. Look what Paul says is the root of the rebellion:

Romans 1:25 - They (sinners) exchanged the truth about God for a lie and worshiped and served the creature rather than the Creator, who is blessed forever! Amen.

There it is. We exchanged the truth about God. Another way to say that would be that we denied the truth about God. We rejected Him as Creator, Master, Provider, Lord. We believed the lie that we, ourselves, were more powerful and worthy of worship. We believe ourselves to be God. We have turned our affections from God, who has made all things, toward the things which God has made. This is a terrible offense against God. So, make no mistake, the reason why human beings are enemies of God is because they have picked the fight.

Why do I bring this up? It's simple: when you consider how God has treated you in comparison to how He should have treated you, it forces your heart to be filled with gratitude and praise! How does one naturally treat enemies? No matter how you answer that question, we can all agree that treating our enemies with kindness is completely counter-intuitive. To love your enemy seems like a contradiction or an error.

God was not under any obligation to love us or treat us with kindness. God owes us nothing. God had no debt to repay. God, for the glory of His name, acted in grace and mercy toward us!

Perhaps you have heard the words "grace" and "mercy" before. Here is a simple definition of these words so we can draw distinction between them and be forever reminded of how incredible our God is!

Grace - to get what you do not deserve.

Mercy - to not get what you do deserve.

God showed us grace by giving us what we absolutely do not deserve and what we are completely unworthy to receive. He gave us Himself. He provided the perfect sacrifice for our sin by taking our guilt upon Himself and paying the debt that we owed. He has given us eternal life through a relationship with Him. Even the smallest of blessings that we enjoy such as the breath that is currently in our lungs, has been given to us by God because of His wonderful grace.

God shows us mercy by not giving us what we deserve. What do we deserve? Hell. His wrath. His righteous anger against our sin. We deserve to be cast away from God forever and treated in accordance with what we deserve. But God has shown great mercy in redirecting His wrath upon Jesus and crushing Jesus for our sin.

If I could sum it up in a simple statement:

God could have silenced His enemies by destroying them. Instead, God saved His enemies by dying for them.

Takeaways from Chapter 8

By nature of our sin, we were not only separated from God, but we were hostile towards Him and set ourselves against Him as His enemies.

God did not do all that He has done for us because we were His friends. God has done all that He has done for us despite us being His enemies.

Grace- to get what you do not deserve.

Mercy- to not get what you do deserve.

God could have silenced His enemies by destroying them. Instead, God saved His enemies by dying for them.

Chapter 9
Our Response

Okay, so, let's say you agree with me on what you have read thus far. I mean, you haven't put the book down yet so perhaps God is working in you right now, and you're curious:

What do I have to do to make this work? How can I be saved?

The problem, once again: God is good, we are not. By nature and choice, we are sinners and are separated from God. Tragically, so many people are deceived into believing that it is our obligation to solve this problem.

Even while Jesus walked the Earth, there was great confusion as to the magnitude of the problem and the ultimate solution.

John 6:28-29 - Then they said to Him, "What must we do, to be doing the works of God?" Jesus answered them, "This is the work of God, **that you believe in him whom He has sent**."

As a minister of the Gospel, and even more so as a Christ-follower, it breaks my heart when people ask the question: "What do I have to do to be right with God?" It is equally as heartbreaking when I see people operate under the misconception that their behaviors that make them right with God. This misunderstanding comes in many forms:

"I just try to live a good life and be a good person."

"I'm not as bad as I used to be and I'm trying to be better."

"I hope God understands."

"When everything is said and done and I stand before God, I think I'll be okay."

It is crucial to our ultimate joy that we understand this truth: There is nothing that must be done by us in order to be made right with God. Everything that needed to be done in order to bring us back into relationship with God was already done by Jesus Christ!

Let me say it again. There is nothing, absolutely nothing, that can or should be done by us because all of the work, all of it, was done by Jesus. Jesus acted on our behalf and did, in completion, what we were unable to do.

Jesus lived the perfect life we needed but could not achieve. Jesus died the death we were condemned to die. Jesus defeated sin, death, Hell, and the grave by rising from the dead.

Since everything has been done and all of the work of redemption has been accomplished, all we are called to do is **believe**.

But, believe what?

First of all, this sounds too good to be true, doesn't it? In many ways, it does sound too good to be true! Paul Washer says it this way:

> "The Gospel is an absolutely unbelievable message...As Christians, we sometimes fail to realize how utterly astounding it is when anyone believes our message." (Regeneration vs. The Idolatry of Decisional Evangelism)

Jesus has done all of the work to save us. We simply believe. But heartbreakingly, many people fail to realize what it is we need to believe.

A lot of people believe in the existence of a cosmic being. Because of the overly-spiritual climate, particularly in America, it is normative for people to be open to the idea of a world that is beyond the physical. Substance abuse recovery programs encourage their participants to rely on a "higher power." Additionally, the concept of "god" is not exclusive to the Christian faith. Major world religions claim the existence of a "god" and even some cults use "god language." Romans 1 tells us that God has plainly revealed Himself in a number of ways. The author, Paul, argues that human beings do not have an acceptable excuse for not knowing God. God has made it obvious that He exists through creation and our conscience; namely, the part of us that seems to innately understand the difference between right and wrong. Perhaps even more alarming is the truth that James, the brother of Jesus, shares with us in James 2:19: "You believe that there is one God. Good! Even the demons believe that--and shudder."

Let's look at **John 6:28-29** again:

> Then they said to Him, "What must we do, to be doing the works of God?" Jesus answered them, **"This is the work of God, that you <u>believe</u> in him whom He has sent."**

It's clear that the kind of belief Jesus calls us to in John 6 is not merely a belief in the existence of a greater cosmic or spiritual being/god. So, exactly what sort of belief is Jesus pointing us to?

Let's zoom in on the verse one more time. This time, let's focus on the object of the belief that Jesus refers to:

> Then they said to Him, "What must we do, to be doing the works of God?" Jesus answered them, **"This is the work of God, that you believe <u>in</u> him whom He has sent."**

Let's clarify who "He" and "Him" are. Who is Jesus talking about? Who is the "Him" that "He" has sent? It's Jesus! Jesus is the "Him"! God the Father is the "He"! Jesus is saying that He was the one whom God had sent!

So, what are we believing? **We are believing that Jesus is who He said He was. We believe that He is the perfect, eternal Son of God and that He is Savior. We believe that He lived a perfect and sinless life. We believe that He died on the cross in our place in order to pay the penalty for our sin. We believe that on the third day He rose again from the dead.**

By believing this, we are fully, freely, and forever forgiven of our sin. Upon our faith in Christ, our sin is paid at the cross, and we are credited with the righteousness of Christ, through faith.

Galatians 2:16 - Yet we know that a person is not justified by works of the law but through faith in Jesus Christ, so we also have believed in Christ Jesus, in order to be justified by faith in Christ and not by works of the law, because by works of the law no one will be justified.

Romans 5:1 - Therefore, since we have been justified by faith, we have peace with God through our Lord Jesus Christ.

Ephesians 2:8-9 - For by grace you have been saved through faith. And this is not your own doing; it is the gift of God, not a result of works, so that no one may boast.

Believe that God is good. Understand that you are not God and you are not good. Believe that God has chosen to glorify Himself by sending His Son, Jesus, to live perfectly, die condemned in your place, and rise again as your Savior. Believe and receive His salvation. **Always remember that the salvation we receive is not a reward for our righteousness but a gift despite our guilt.**

Takeaways from Chapter 9

It is crucial for our ultimate joy and our understanding of the Gospel that we cherish this truth: There is nothing that must be done by us in order to be made right with God.

We are believing that Jesus is who He said He was. We believe that He is the perfect, eternal Son of God and that He is Savior. We believe that He lived a perfect and sinless life. We believe that He died on the cross in our place in order to pay the penalty for our sin. We believe that on the third day, He rose again from the dead.

Always remember that the salvation we receive is not a reward for our righteousness but a gift despite our guilt.

Chapter <u>10</u>

Saved

As Christians, we use a common phraseology: saved. We say: Jesus saves! We say: I have been saved by God! We say: Jesus is the only way that anyone can be saved!

I passionately agree with all of those statements. However, I would simply like to expound on those thoughts and form them into complete ideas.

Saved from what?

We have been saved from our sin! We were once dead in our sin. We were slaves to our sin and held captive by it. God, in Christ, has saved us and rescued us from ourselves! Our sin leads us only into rebellion, and if one dies in their sin, they go into eternity separated from God. **But God has saved us by paying the sin debt we owed. By giving us Jesus Christ's righteousness as a gift through faith, He has brought us into His Kingdom and family!**

Saved by Who?

God! We have not saved ourselves. **All of the credit for our salvation belongs to God alone!** We were absolutely incapable of solving our sin problem on our own. God has done it all, and all of the glory belongs to Him!

Saved why?

We have been saved for the glory of God! The Bible teaches us that God does everything He does in order that He might be glorified. God is more passionate about His fame than anything else. God has chosen to glorify Himself through the creation, pursuit, and redemption of His people.

Saved in order to do what?

We have been saved in order to testify to the goodness and grace of God! As objects of His mercy, we are to gladly worship Him and praise Him for who He is and what He has done! Now, because the Holy Spirit dwells in us, we carry the message of the Gospel with us to the ends of the earth in order to see people become reconciled to God through faith in Jesus Christ!

We were not redirected toward better things but resurrected into a new life.

Saved for sure?

Can we know for sure that we are saved? How can we have a confidence in knowing our salvation is legitimate?

Throughout my years of serving as a pastor (in various capacities), I have seen a certain type of behavior repeatedly. I've noticed people so insecure in their salvation they shackle themselves to tradition and superstition in order to make themselves feel more at ease in the moment.

To illustrate this point, meet Ray.

Meet Ray

Ray put his faith in Christ for salvation years ago. The Holy Spirit moved in Ray's life and revealed to Him the holiness of God, his need for a Savior, the sufficiency of the work of Jesus Christ, and the need for faith and repentance. Ray sincerely believed the message of the Gospel and surrendered to follow Jesus Christ.

Over the next several months, Ray became extremely passionate about the things of God. He was hungry to read God's Word and fell more and more in love with his local church and his brothers and sisters who attended with him. Ray felt as though every sermon, every blurb in his daily devotional book, and every worship song was meant directly for him and his current situation.

After a few months, his enthusiasm began to fade. He was ashamed to admit it, but he started to lose interest. It became harder and harder to keep his attention on the things of God. As he sat in church one day, he did all he could in order to direct his focus on the pastor's sermon.

Ray's dwindling passion began to produce guilt in his spirit. He began comparing himself to other believers. Every time someone in his church expressed joy in Christ, Ray began to feel as though something was wrong with him because he no longer experienced such joy.

One day, the guilt became too much. The pastor spoke about living a life in total surrender toward Christ. "That's it," Ray thought, "maybe I just never fully believed!" So, at the end of the message, Ray went forward to receive Christ again. But in Ray's mind, this time, it was the real thing. He had found his passion again. He had become reenergized. He felt as though He was closer to Christ than ever before! Whenever someone asked him to share his testimony, he shared about how he had given his life to Christ once but had simply gone through the motions. He explained how he truly gave his life to Christ a second time and only then did he truly understand what he was doing.

Things seemed to improve until old habits from Ray's past began to make their way back into his life. He had replaced his sinful habits with "Christian" habits, but he found that he could only distract himself for so long before he found himself indulging in things that brought him pleasure before he became a Christian. He had the perfect rationalization in his mind: "No one is perfect!" But soon, his "once in a while" struggles turned into "quite often" which then became "every available opportunity" and eventually led to "this is too powerful to resist...this is a part of me."

But it wouldn't be long until a worship song contained lyrics that struck a chord in Ray's heart. He found himself to be overly emotional during a church service one day. The worship was phenomenal and the message seemed to include details from his life. So, once again, at the end of the message when the pastor asked people to stand and come forward to receive

Christ, Ray felt compelled once again to stand and walk to the front of the church. When confronted as to why he came forward, Ray utilized the ultra-popular Christian verbiage, "I feel like I need to rededicate my life."

Several years go by, and several more rededications. Ray is determined not to allow any opportunity to pass him by. He wants to leave nothing to question. Every time the pastor encourages people to take some sort of action (stand, raise their hand, come forward, etc.) to receive Christ, Ray complies. Every time the pastor leads people in a prayer to receive Christ, Ray repeats the words. Every time the church holds a baptism service, Ray gets into the water.

What's the problem with this? Is there a problem?

What is obvious from Ray's behavior, namely his constant need to "be saved" over and over, is that Ray does not truly understand what it means to be saved. Ray is operating under the lie that salvation is because of him and that it depends on him.

If I were Ray's pastor, or even his brother in Christ, here is how I would encourage him. Also, in the case that you find yourself in a similar position as Ray, my desire is to encourage you as well.

As Christians, we are saved because of what Jesus has done, not because of what we do. Our salvation is something that happens to us, not because of us. **God did not choose to save you because of anything good in you, therefore He is not depending on anything good from you to keep you saved.**

Philippians 1:6 - And I am sure of this, that **he (God) who began a good work in you (salvation) will bring it to completion** at the day of Jesus Christ.

There are two halves to the truth found in this verse: God began the work of salvation in you, and He will finish the work He began! **We can have assurance in salvation because God has promised to keep us. This is such an important truth. In salvation, it is not the Christian who is responsible for holding onto God, but rather, it is God who is responsible for holding onto the Christian. This means you are not saved because of your faithfulness but because of God's faithfulness.**

Romans 8:29-30 - For those whom he foreknew he also predestined to be conformed to the image of his Son, in order that he might be the firstborn among many brothers. And those whom he predestined he also called, and those whom he called he also justified, and those whom he justified he also glorified.

There, in verses 29 and 30 of Romans 8, is what those who study the Bible refer to as the "golden chain of redemption." Imagine a thread between the first divine act of God toward the believer and the last. God **foreknows, predestines, calls, justifies,** and **glorifies** the believer. All of these actions are done by God, and nothing can thwart the purposes of God in completing the work He begins in the believer. Just a few verses later in Romans 8, Paul rounds out his argument with this glorious rhetorical question:

Romans 8:33-35 - Who shall bring any charge against God's elect? **It is God who justifies.** Who is to condemn? Christ Jesus is the one who died—more than that, who was raised—who is at the right hand of God, who indeed is interceding for us. **Who shall separate us from the love of Christ?**

Takeaways from Chapter 10

But God has saved us by paying the sin debt that we owed and by giving us Jesus Christ's righteousness as a gift, through faith and has brought us into His Kingdom and family!

All of the credit for our salvation belongs to God alone!

We were not redirected towards better things but resurrected into a new life.

We can have assurance in salvation because God has promised to keep us. This is such an important truth. In salvation, it is not the Christian who is responsible for holding onto God, but rather it is God who is responsible for holding onto the Christian. This means that you are not saved because of your faithfulness, but because of God's faithfulness.

God did not choose to save you because of anything good in you, therefore He is not depending anything good from to keep you saved.

Credits

All of the glory for this project belongs to Jesus Christ. It is by His grace that I have been given this opportunity to present the Gospel in a way that I hope many will understand and respond to.

My wife, Stephanie, has been such an anchor of support and wisdom in my life. I am so blessed to be able to enjoy the good gifts of God in my life, and I gladly share them all with her.

God has used so many men to shape my understanding of Scripture and, ultimately, my life as a believer. Below is a list of some those men. If you are someone who desires to know God more deeply and grow in your understanding of the Gospel of Jesus Christ, I would highly encourage you to glean from their wisdom and teaching. God has used them to teach me much of what I have come to understand about theology, the Christian faith, and Scripture.

Matt Chandler - Pastor, The Village Church, TX

John Piper - Founder, Desiring God

J.D. Greear - Pastor, The Summit Church, NC. President, Southern Baptist Convention

Mark Driscoll - Pastor, The Trinity Church, Scottsdale, AZ

David Platt - Pastor, Author

Voddie Baucham - Pastor, Author

Dr. James White - Christian Apologist, Author, Director of Alpha & Omega Ministries

Jeff Durbin - Pastor, Apologia Church, Tempe, AZ

John MacArthur - Pastor, Author

R.C. Sproul - Pastor, Author, Founder of Ligonier Ministries

Paul Washer - Evangelist

ABOUT THE AUTHOR

David Rotteveel is a Christ-follower, husband, father, pastor, and public speaker. God has given him a passion for sharing the message of the Gospel and seeing people come into a relationship with God through Jesus Christ. Some of David's favorite pastimes are serving the local church, playing and watching sports, and spending time with his family. He is married to the love of his life, Stephanie. Together, they have two children, Cadence (6) and Luke (3).